Higher Ground

Songs That Lift the Spirit

Arranged for Solo Piano by Victor Labenske

CONTENTS

Higher Ground

I'm pressing on the upward way;
New heights I'm gaining every day,
Still praying as I'm onward bound,
"Lord, plant my feet on higher ground."

Refrain
Lord, lift me up and let me stand,
By faith, on heaven's tableland.
A higher plane than I have found–
Lord, plant my feet on higher ground.

My heart has no desire to stay
Where doubts arise and fears dismay.
Though some may dwell where these abound,
My prayer, my aim is higher ground.
Refrain

I want to live above the world,
Though Satan's darts at me are hurled;
For faith has caught the joyful sound,
The song of saints on higher ground.
Refrain

I want to scale the utmost height,
And catch a gleam of glory bright;
But still I'll pray till heaven I've found,
"Lord, lead me on to higher ground."
Refrain

In memory of Dr. Dana Walling

Higher Ground

JOHNSON OATMAN, JR.

CHARLES L. GABRIEL
Arranged by Victor Labenske

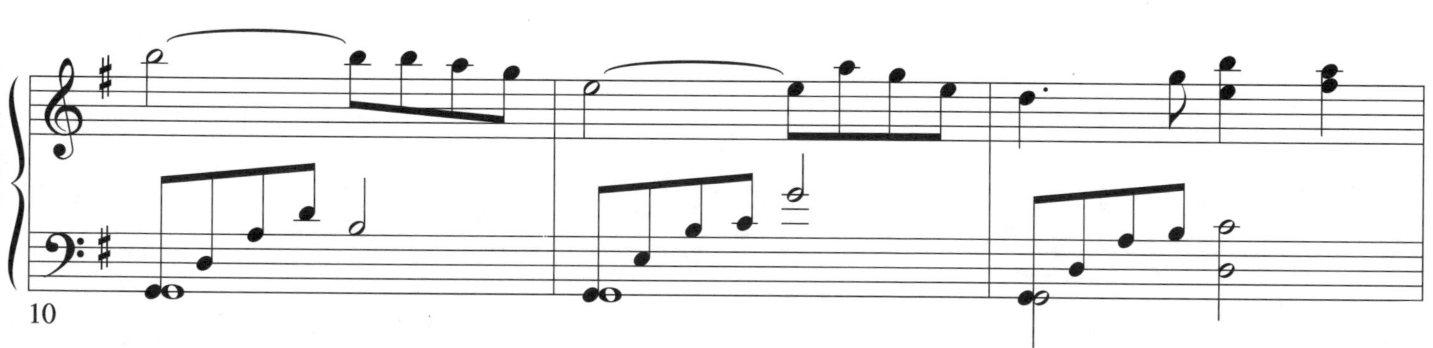

"My heart has no desire to stay..."
mp
13
16
19
cresc.
22
mf
"A higher plane..."
rit.
25

cresc.
a tempo
f
decresc.
rit.
28
8va
p
a tempo
31
sfp
34
"I want to live above the world..."
Confidently ♩ = ca. 100
rit.
mp
37
"...Satan's darts at me are hurled.."
"For faith has caught the joyful sound..."
cresc.
mf
40

43
a tempo
f
decresc.
mf
rit.
46
a tempo
f
mf
6
6
8vb
49
f
52
rit.
a tempo
mp
rit.
poco accel.
55
rit.
a tempo

rit.
a tempo
cresc.
rit.
8vb
58
Triumphantly ♩ = ca. 108
"...and catch a gleam of glory bright;"
f
sub. mf
cresc.
3
61
"But still I'll pray..."
8va
Slower ♩ = ca. 92
ff
f
molto rit.
mf
64
cresc.
67
70

A little faster ♩ = ca. 96
f
73
76
mp
Slower
79
accel. poco a poco
cresc.
82
f
mp
cresc.
rit.
8va
ff
85

Arise, My Soul, Arise

Arise, my soul, arise.
Shake off thy guilty fears.
The bleeding Sacrifice
In my behalf appears.
Before the throne my Surety stands,
Before the throne my Surety stands;
My name is written on His hands.

Five bleeding wounds He bears,
Received on Calvary.
They pour effectual prayers;
They strongly plead for me.
"Forgive him, O forgive," they cry.
"Forgive him, O forgive," they cry,
"Nor let that ransomed sinner die."

My God is reconciled;
His pardoning voice I hear.
He owns me for His child;
I can no longer fear.
With confidence I now draw nigh,
With confidence I now draw nigh,
And, "Father, Abba, Father," cry.

Arise, My Soul, Arise

CHARLES WESLEY

LEWIS EDSON
Arranged by Victor Labenske

16
poco rit. e decresc.
mp
a tempo
19
cresc.
mf
mp
23
26
mf
Ped.
8va
rit. e decresc.
"Five bleeding wounds He bears..."
A little faster ♩. = ca. 100
mp
29

32
35
"Five bleeding wounds He bears..."
mf
38
41
44
mp
decresc.

"'Forgive him, O forgive', they cry..."
Tempo I
p
mel.
mf
47
mel.
mf
p
mel.
mf
p
50
cresc.
53
"My God is reconciled..."
f
56
60

8va
"With confidence I now draw nigh..."
sub. mp
cresc.
poco rit.
a tempo
mf
63
Ped.
66
cresc.
f
70
74
cresc.
poco rit.
a tempo
ff
poco accel.
78
rit.
(♮)
8va

Savior, like a Shepherd Lead Us

Savior, like a shepherd lead us;
Much we need Thy tender care.
In Thy pleasant pastures feed us;
For our use Thy folds prepare.
Blessed Jesus, blessed Jesus!
Thou hast bought us; Thine we are.
Blessed Jesus, blessed Jesus!
Thou hast bought us; Thine we are.

He Leadeth Me

He leadeth me! O blessed thought!
O words with heavenly comfort fraught!
Whate'er I do, where'er I be,
Still 'tis God's hand that leadeth me.

Refrain
He leadeth me; He leadeth me.
By His own hand He leadeth me.
His faithful follower I would be,
For by His hand He leadeth me.

Where He Leads Me

I can hear my Savior calling;
I can hear my Savior calling;
I can hear my Savior calling,
"Take thy cross and follow, follow Me."

Refrain
Where He leads me I will follow;
Where He leads me I will follow;
Where He leads me I will follow;
I'll go with Him, with Him all the way.

In memory of Betty Watson

He Leads Me Medley

Savior, like a Shepherd Lead Us*
He Leadeth Me**
Where He Leads Me***

Arranged by Victor Labenske

*Words attr. to Dorothy A. Thrupp; Music by William B. Bradbury.
**Words by Joseph H. Gilmore; Music by William B. Bradbury.
***Words by E. W. Blandy; Music by John S. Norris.

13
15
f
17
19
rit.
mp
22
Slower ♩ = ca. 66
l.h.
Suddenly faster ♩ = ca. 84
p

"He leadeth me! O blessed thought..."
pp
mf
25
28
30
33
35
mf

37
39
rit. e decresc.
a tempo
p
42
rit.
mf
p
mf
45
a tempo
mp
48
mf
decresc.
rit.

"I can hear my Savior calling..."
Slower ♩ = ca. 72
p
51
54
cresc.
mf
57
p
molto rit.
accel. e cresc.
"Where He leads me I will follow..."
With devotion ♩ = ca. 76
mel.
mf
61

63

cresc.

f

"I'll go with Him..."

65

rit.

mf

8va

Slower ♩ = ca. 63

mp

67

8va

69

p

8va

8va

mp

rit.

p

71

There Is a Redeemer

There is a Redeemer– Jesus, God's own Son,
Precious Lamb of God, Messiah, Holy One.

Refrain
Thank You, O my Father, for giving us Your Son,
And leaving Your Spirit till the work on earth is done.

Jesus, my Redeemer, name above all names,
Precious Lamb of God, Messiah, O for sinners slain.
Refrain

When I stand in Glory, I will see His face;
There I'll serve my King forever in that holy place.
Refrain

There Is a Redeemer

Words and Music by
MELODY GREEN
Arranged by Victor Labenske

Thankfully ♩ = ca. 126

"There is a Redeemer– Jesus, God's own Son..."

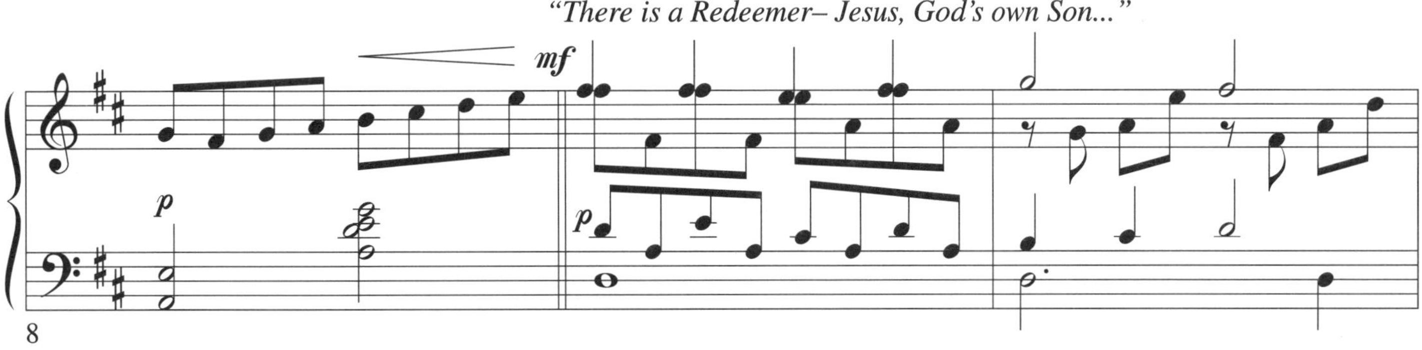

decresc.
p
cresc.
mf
mf
p
rit.
a tempo
p
cresc.
14
17
20
23
26

mf
29

"Jesus, my Redeemer, name above all names..."
p
mel.
mf
33

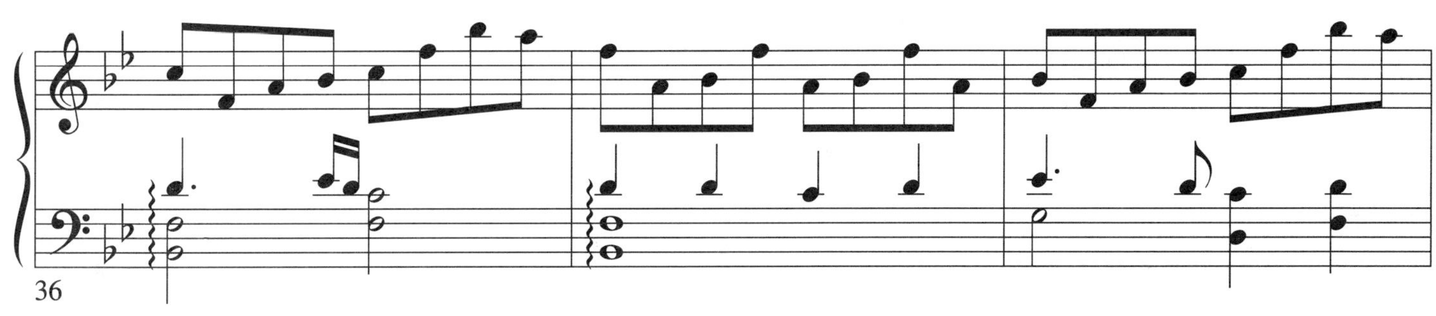
36

mel.
rit.
a tempo
mf
39

42

p
mel.
mf
rit.
45

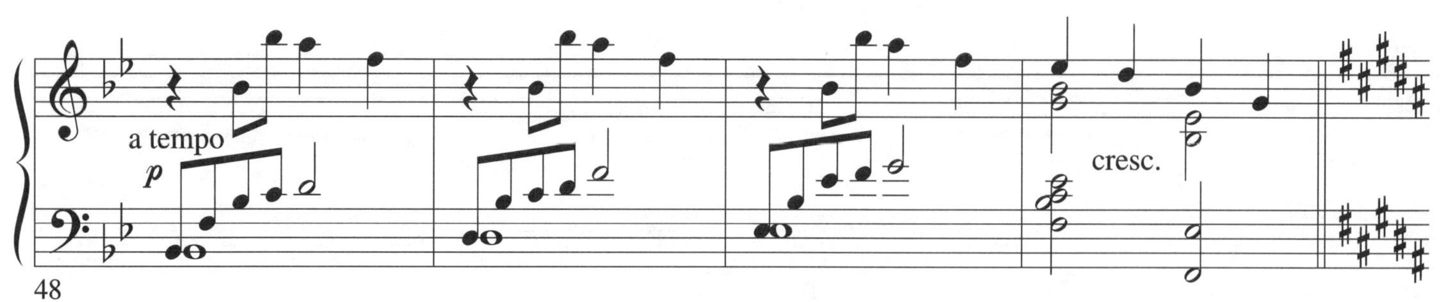
a tempo
p
cresc.
48

mf
rit. e cresc.
52

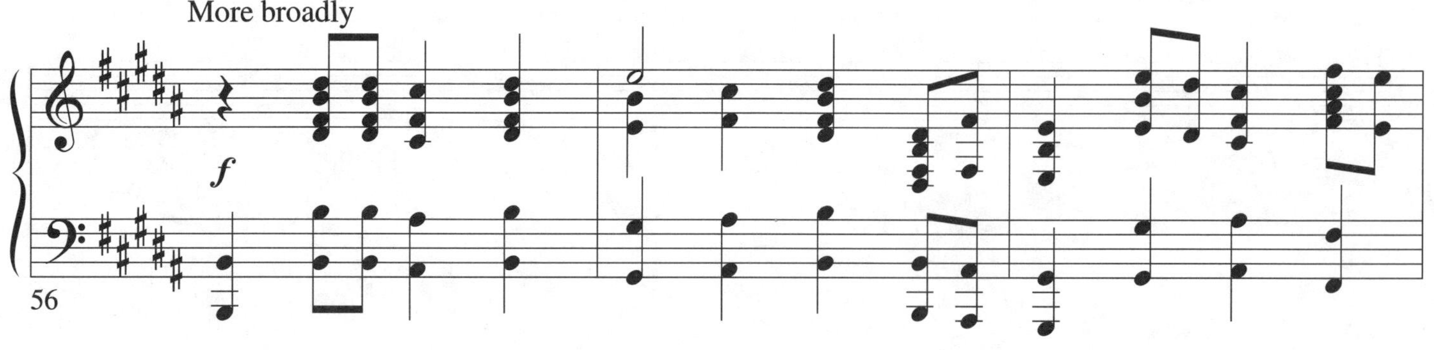
"When I stand in Glory, I will see His face..."
More broadly
f
56

59

cresc.
f
mf
decresc.
mp
decresc.
p
rit.
8va
62
65
69
72
75

When Morning Gilds the Skies

When morning gilds the skies,
My heart awaking cries:
May Jesus Christ be praised!
Alike at work and prayer,
To Jesus I repair.
May Jesus Christ be praised!

The night becomes as day
When from the heart we say:
May Jesus Christ be praised!
The powers of darkness fear
When this sweet chant they hear:
May Jesus Christ be praised!

Be this, while life is mine,
My canticle divine:
May Jesus Christ be praised!
Be this the eternal song
Through all the ages long:
May Jesus Christ be praised!

When Morning Gilds the Skies

Katholisches Gesangbuch

JOSEPH BARNBY
Arranged by Victor Labenske

With awe ♩ = ca. 132

(8va)
16
cresc.
rit.
mf
a tempo
20
23
decresc. e rit.
p
a tempo
26
pp
29

"The night becomes as day..."
rit.
p
gradually a tempo
cresc.
32

"May Jesus Christ be praised..."
f
36

"The powers of darkness fear..."
mf
p
cresc.
39

poco rit.
f
43

a tempo
mf
46

49
cresc.
f
52
rit.
"Be this while life is mine..."
Broadly
55
59
8vb
62

65
mf
68
cresc.
rit.
f
a tempo
71
cresc.
74
f
77
cresc. e rit.
ff
8va
8vb
Ped.

’Tis So Sweet to Trust in Jesus

’Tis so sweet to trust in Jesus,
Just to take Him at His Word,
Just to rest upon His promise,
Just to know: “Thus saith the Lord.”

Refrain
Jesus, Jesus, how I trust Him!
How I’ve proved Him o’er and o’er!
Jesus, Jesus, precious Jesus!
O for grace to trust Him more!

Yes, ’tis sweet to trust in Jesus,
Just from sin and self to cease,
Just from Jesus simply taking
Life and rest, and joy and peace.
Refrain

I’m so glad I learned to trust Thee,
Precious Jesus, Savior, Friend;
And I know that Thou art with me,
Wilt be with me to the end.
Refrain

'Tis So Sweet to Trust in Jesus

LOUISA M. R. STEAD

WILLIAM J. KIRKPATRICK
Arranged by Victor Labenske

Black gospel style ♩. = ca. 48

A little faster ♩. = ca. 52
mf with a steady beat
rit.
15
19
22
26
29

With energy ♩ = ca. 160

f

33

8vb

36

8vb

39

"Yes, 'tis sweet to trust in Jesus..."

42

45

48
mf
51
3
54
57
f
3
60
5

63
8vb
66
(♮)
69
mf
73
8vb
f
77

"I'm so glad I learned to trust Thee..."
80
8vb
83
8vb
86
89
92
3

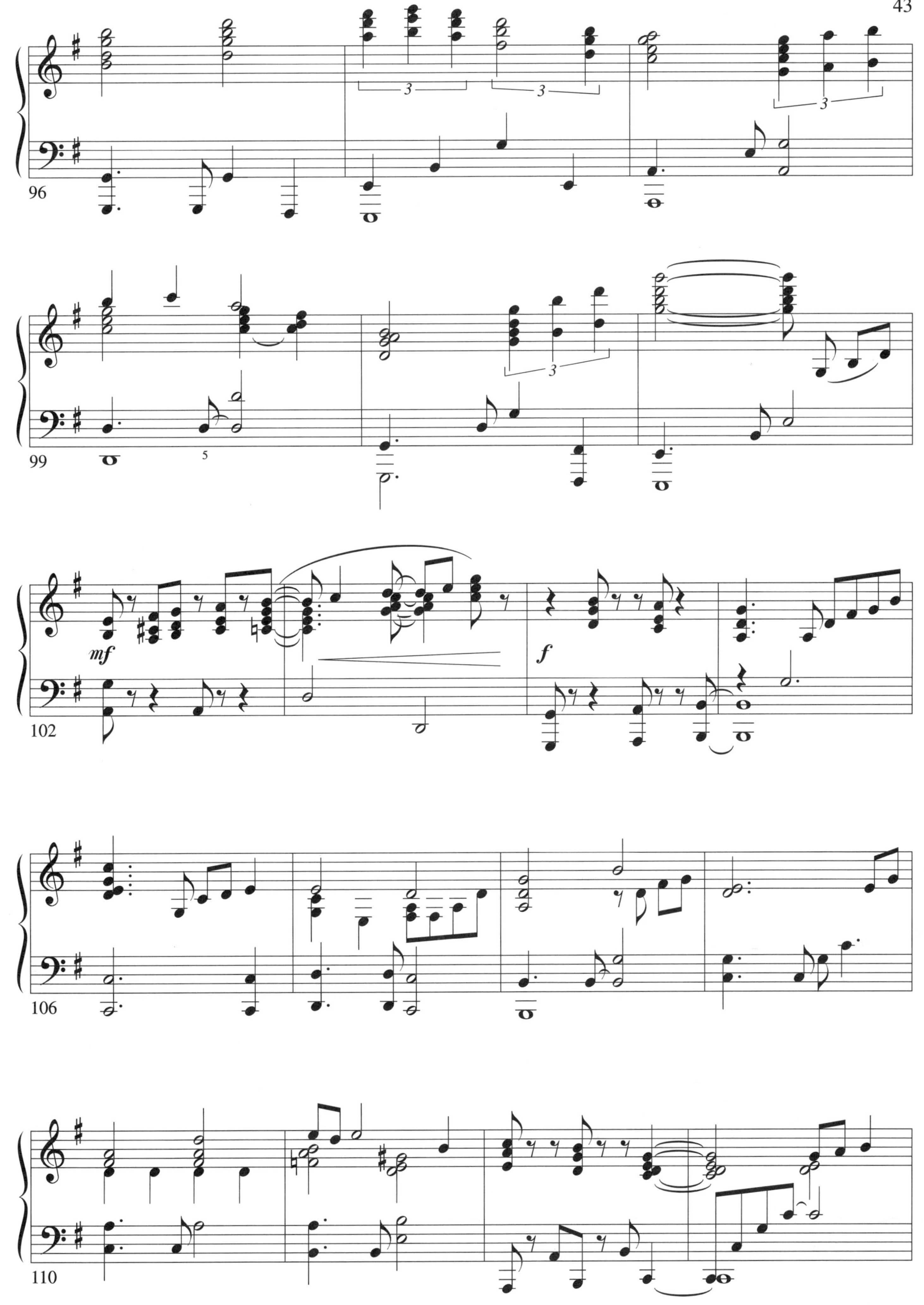

96
99
5
102
mf
f
106
110

mp cresc.
114
Ped. ✽ no pedal

f
mp cresc.
118
Ped. ✽ no pedal

f
122
with pedal

126

8va
3
6
6
rit.
129
Ped.

Rejoice, the Lord Is King

Rejoice, the Lord is King;
Your Lord and King adore!
Rejoice, give thanks, and sing,
And triumph evermore.
Lift up your heart;
Lift up your voice!
Rejoice; again I say: rejoice!

All Hail the Power of Jesus' Name

All hail the power of Jesus' name!
Let angels prostrate fall.
Bring forth the royal diadem,
And crown Him Lord of all.
Bring forth the royal diadem,
And crown Him Lord of all.

Jesus Shall Reign

Jesus shall reign where'er the sun
Does his successive journeys run;
His kingdom spread from shore to shore,
Till moons shall wax and wane no more.

Crown Him with Many Crowns

Crown Him with many crowns,
The Lamb upon His throne.
Hark! how the heavenly anthem drowns
All music but its own!
Awake, my soul, and sing
Of Him who died for thee,
And hail Him as thy matchless King
Through all eternity.

Jesus the King Medley

Rejoice the Lord Is King*
All Hail the Power of Jesus' Name**
Jesus Shall Reign***
Crown Him with Many Crowns****

Arranged by Victor Labenske

Triumphantly ♩ = ca. 96

ff

3

6

* Words by Charles Wesley; Music by John Darwall.
**Words by Edward Perronet; Music by Oliver Holden.
***Words by Isaac Watts; Music by John Hatton.
****Words by Matthew Bridges and Godfrey Thring; Music by George J. Elvey.

10
12
15
"Rejoice, the Lord is King..."
Slightly faster ♩= ca. 108
mf
18
f
mf
21

f
mf
25
28
Tempo I
rit.
f
30
32
“All hail the power of Jesus’ name...”
Slightly faster ♩= ca. 108
mf
35

38
p
mf
41
cresc.
44
f
mp
mf
8vb
47
cresc.
rit.
Tempo I
f
50
rit. e decresc.

"Jesus shall reign..."
Slightly faster ♩ = ca. 108
mp
53
56
cresc.
59
f
62
65
cresc. e rit.

Tempo I ♩= ca. 96
ff
68
"Crown Him with many crowns..."
Slightly faster ♩= ca. 104
rit.
f a tempo
71
74
7
7
77
80

84
87
90
rit.
Tempo I ♩ = ca. 96
93
8va
rit.
8vb

Joyful, Joyful, We Adore Thee

Joyful, joyful, we adore Thee,
God of glory, Lord of love;
Hearts unfold like flowers before Thee,
Opening to the sun above.
Melt the clouds of sin and sadness;
Drive the dark of doubt away.
Giver of immortal gladness,
Fill us with the light of day!

All Thy works with joy surround Thee;
Earth and heaven reflect Thy rays.
Stars and angels sing around Thee,
Center of unbroken praise.
Field and forest, vale and mountain,
Flowery meadow, flashing sea,
Chanting bird and flowing fountain
Call us to rejoice in Thee!

Thou art giving and forgiving,
Ever blessing, ever blest,
Wellspring of the joy of living,
Ocean depth of happy rest!
Thou our Father, Christ our Brother–
All who live in love are Thine.
Teach us how to love each other;
Lift us to the joy divine!

Mortals join the mighty chorus
Which the morning stars began.
Father-love is reigning o'er us;
Brother-love binds man to man.
Ever singing, march we onward,
Victors in the midst of strife.
Joyful music leads us sunward
In the triumph song of life!

Joyful, Joyful, We Adore Thee

HENRY VAN DYKE

LUDWIG VAN BEETHOVEN
Arranged by Victor Labenske

*If necessary, play at a slower tempo keeping eighth note constant throughout.

"Melt the clouds of sin and sadness..."
f
Ped.
8va
mf
decresc.
p
mf

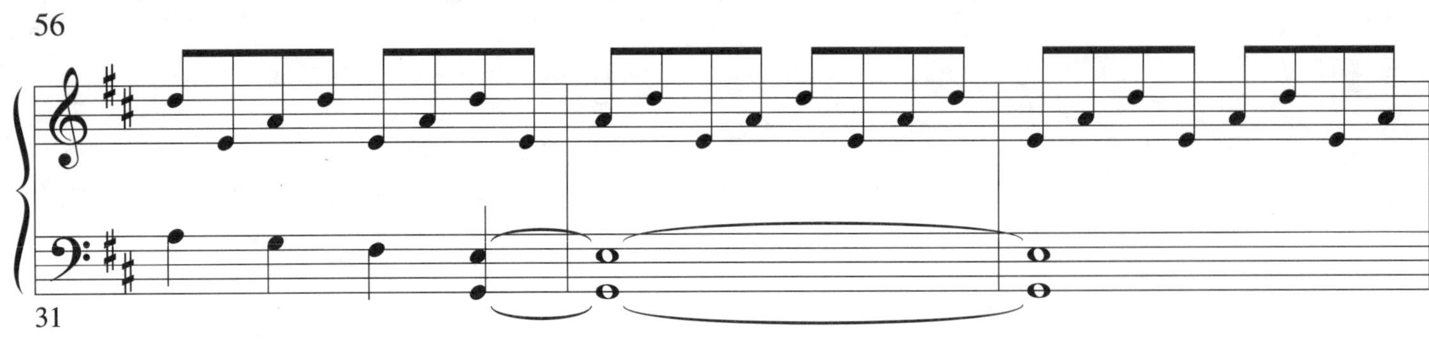

"All Thy works with joy surround Thee..."

mp
46

sub. mp
49

52

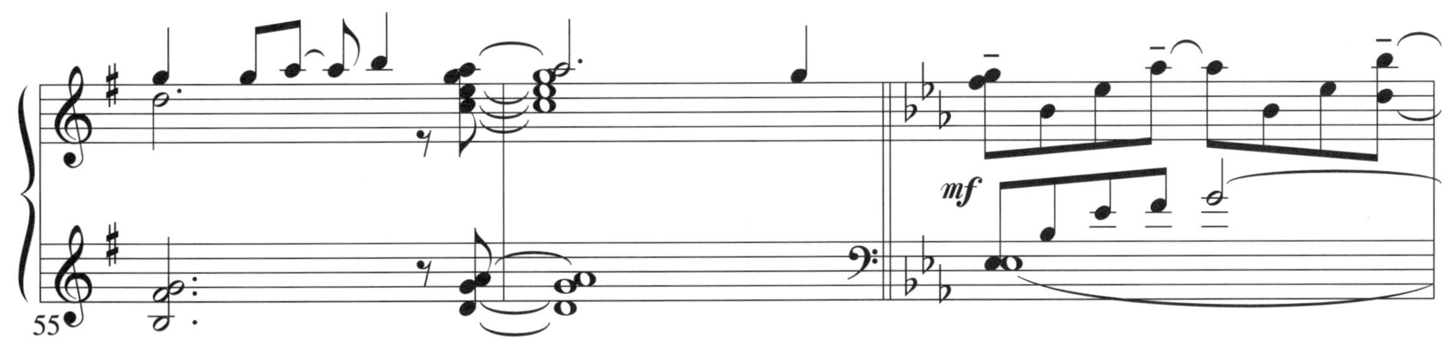

mf
55

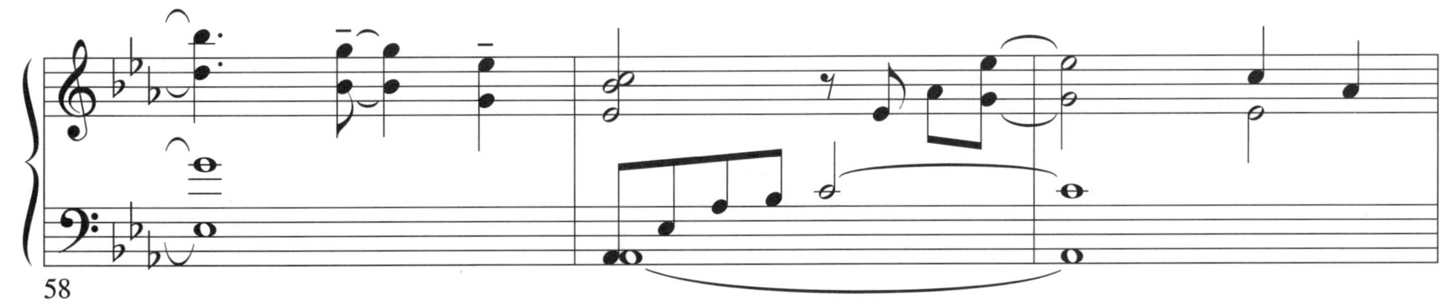

58

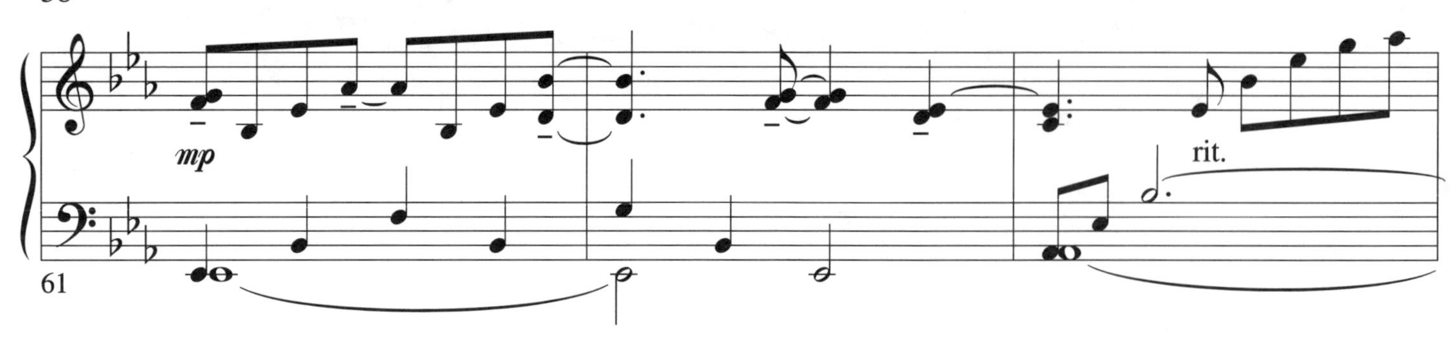
mp
rit.
61

"Thou art giving and forgiving..."
Slower ♩ = ca. 138
64

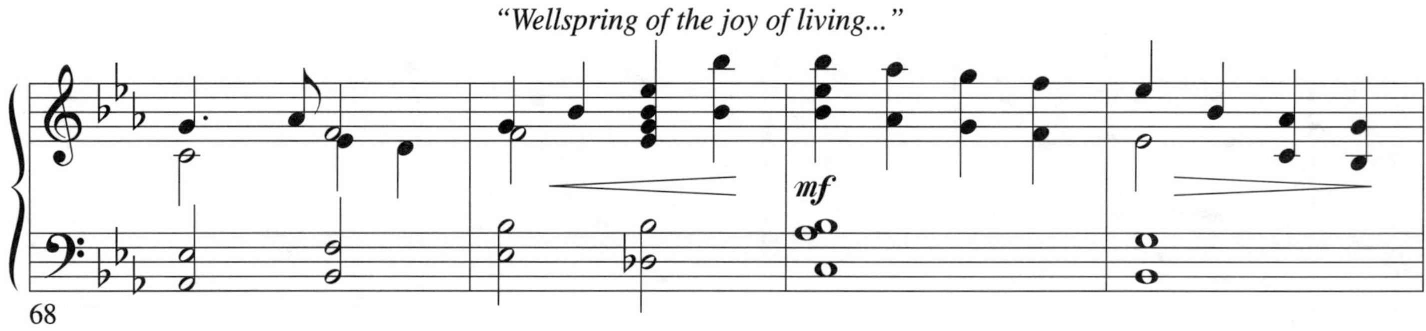
"Wellspring of the joy of living..."
mf
68

mp
sub. p
72

mf
rit.
p
76

"Teach us how to love each other..."
a tempo
rit.
80
Ped.

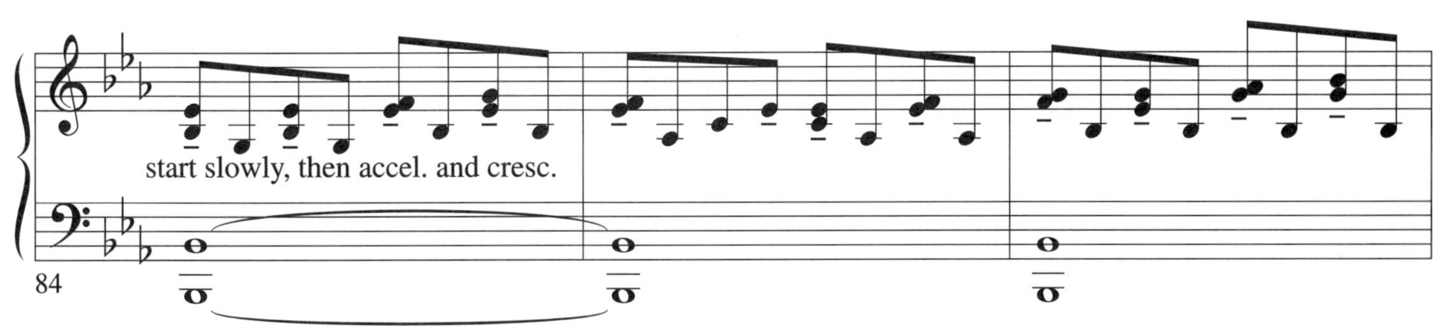
start slowly, then accel. and cresc.
84

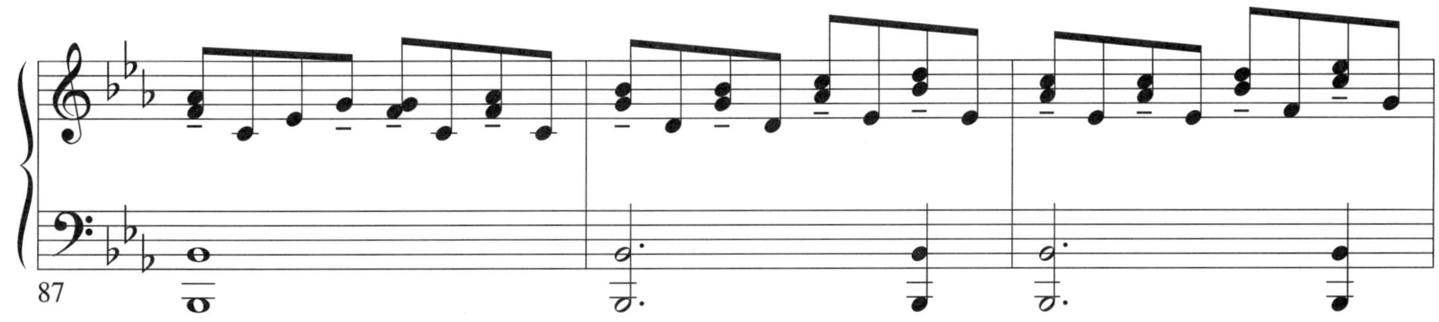
87

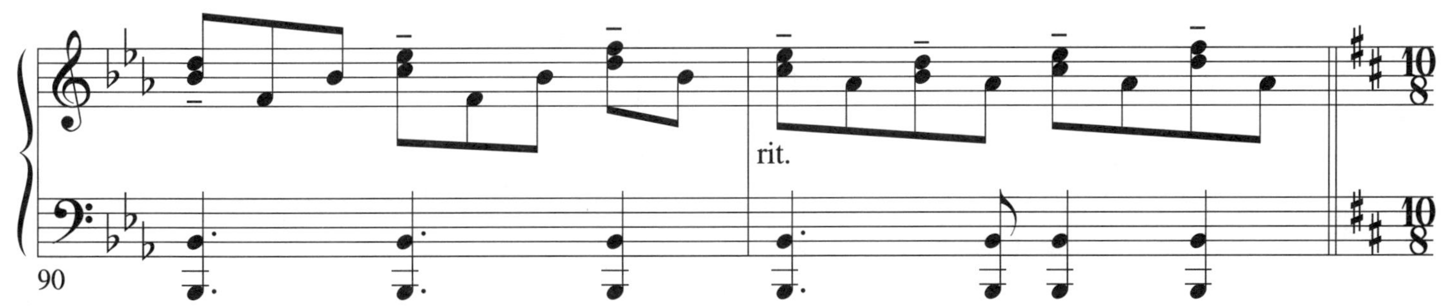
rit.
90

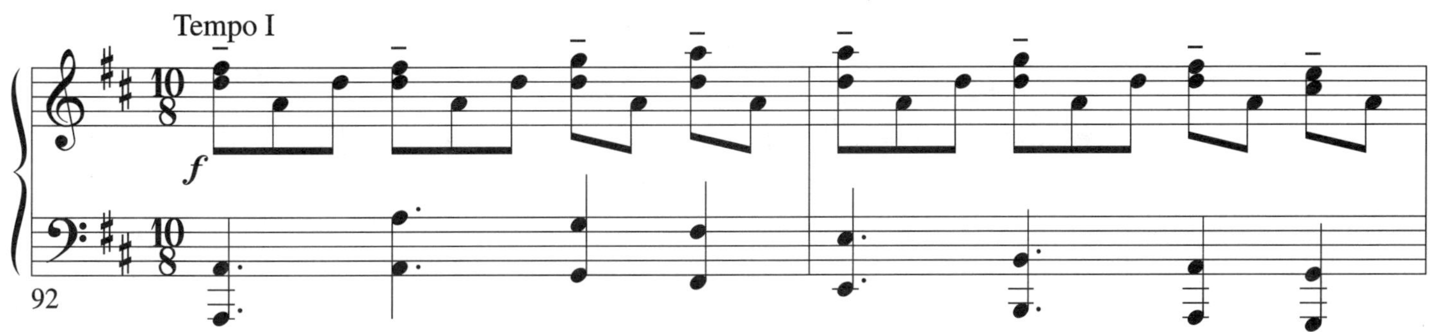
"Mortals join the mighty chorus..."
Tempo I
f
92

94
8vb
97
8va
mf
100
(8va)
mp cresc.
103
f
106

108
sfp
cresc. poco a poco
110
112
f
cresc.
114
117
1
1
1
8va
ff
8vb

When We All Get to Heaven

Sing the wondrous love of Jesus;
Sing His mercy and His grace.
In the mansions, bright and blessed,
He'll prepare for us a place.

Refrain
When we all get to heaven,
What a day of rejoicing that will be!
When we all see Jesus,
We'll sing and shout the victory!

While we walk the pilgrim pathway,
Clouds will overspread the sky;
But when travelling days are over,
Not a shadow, not a sigh!
Refrain

Let us then be true and faithful,
Trusting, serving every day.
Just one glimpse of Him in glory
Will the toils of life repay.
Refrain

Onward to the prize before us!
Soon His beauty we'll behold.
Soon the pearly gates will open;
We shall tread the streets of gold.
Refrain

When We All Get to Heaven

ELIZA E. HEWITT

EMILY D. WILSON
Arranged by Victor Labenske

3
3
12
f
3
14
16
3
18
mf
20

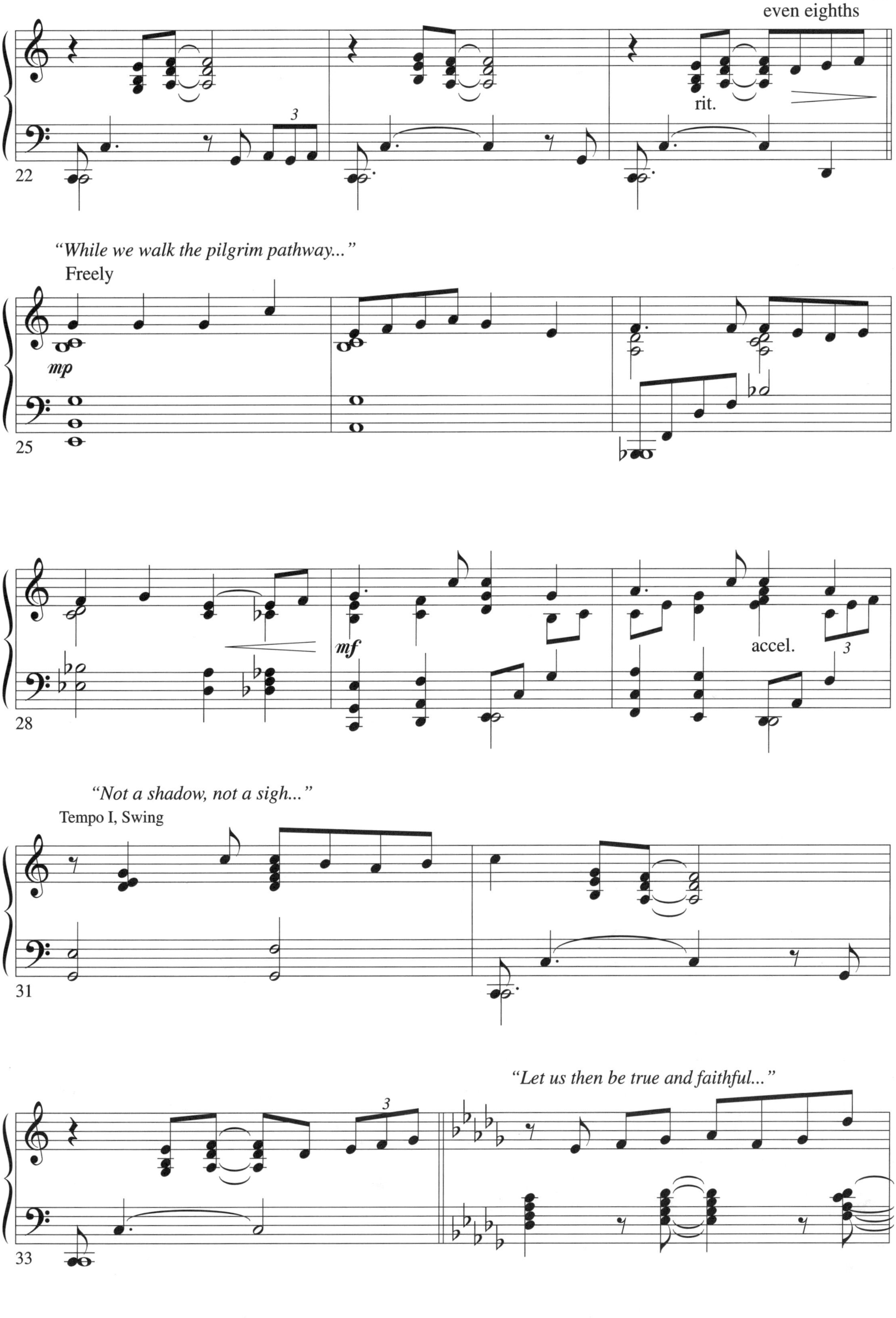

even eighths

rit.

22

"While we walk the pilgrim pathway..."

Freely

mp

25

mf

accel.

28

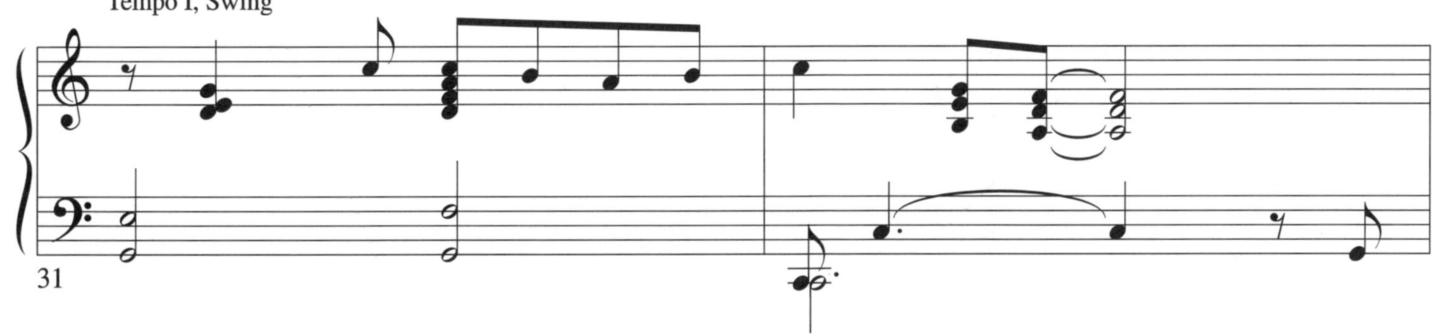

35
37
39
41
43

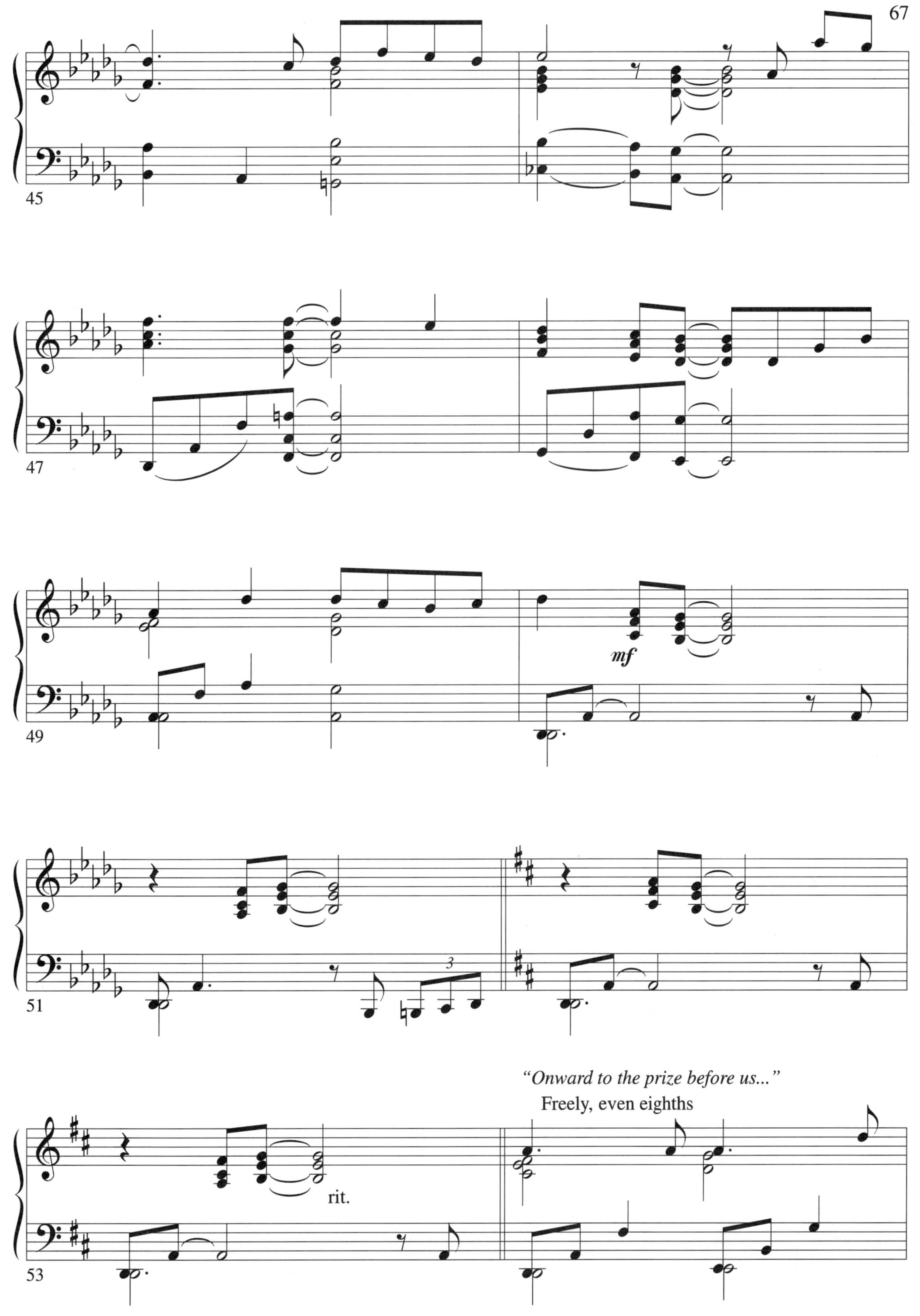
45
47
49
mf
51
3
"Onward to the prize before us..."
Freely, even eighths
rit.
53

poco rit.
a tempo
rit.
55
a tempo
poco rit.
a tempo
58
Tempo I Swing
61
63
65

3
67
mf
cresc.
69
8va
f
71
mf
cresc.
73
8va
white key gliss.
ff
75
8vb
Ped.
*

America, the Beautiful

O beautiful for spacious skies,
For amber waves of grain,
For purple mountain majesties
Above the fruited plain!
America! America!
God shed His grace on thee,
And crown thy good with brotherhood
From sea to shining sea!

The Star-spangled Banner

O say, can you see, by the dawn's early light,
What so proudly we hailed at the twilight's last gleaming?
Whose broad stripes and bright stars, through the perilous fight,
O'er the ramparts we watched, were so gallantly streaming?
And the rocket's red glare, the bombs bursting in air
Gave proof through the night that our flag was still there.
O say, does that star-spangled banner yet wave
O'er the land of the free and the home of the brave?

My Country, 'Tis of Thee

My country, 'tis of thee,
Sweet land of liberty,
Of thee I sing:
Land where my fathers died,
Land of the Pilgrims' pride,
From every mountainside
Let freedom ring!

America! Medley

America, the Beautiful*
The Star-spangled Banner**
My Country, 'Tis of Thee***

Arranged by Victor Labenske

*Words by Katharine Lee Bates; Music by Samuel A. Ward.
**Words by Francis Scott Key; Music attr. to John Stafford Smith.
***Words by Samuel F. Smith; Music, *Thesaurus Musicus.*

13
rit.
a tempo
16
19
cresc.
22
accel.
Faster ♩ = ca. 126
25

27
30
33
36
39
rit.
Freely
mf

42
Ped.
44
Ped.
rit. e cresc.
46
"O say can you see..."
f
With feeling ♩ = ca. 104
48
51

mp
3
f
mf
f
mf
mp
pp
54
57
60
63
66

69
71
73
75
77
cresc.
mp

cresc.
79
mf
cresc.
82
f
86
90
93

95
98
cresc.
rit.
101
7
8va
ff
f
103
sub. mp
a tempo
106

cresc.
108
110
rit.
"My country, 'tis of thee..."
a tempo
f
112
115
118

121
124
127
rit.
a tempo
cresc.
130
rit.
132
ff
8va
Ped.